Presents

Learn Piano 1
The Method for a New Generation

1

Written & Method By:
John McCarthy

Adapted By: Jimmy Rutkowski
Supervising Editor: Joe Palombo
Music Transcribing & Engraving: Jimmy Rutkowski
Production Manager: Joe Palombo
Layout, Graphics & Design: Jimmy Rutkowski, Rodney Dabney
Photography: Jimmy Rutkowski
Copy Editor: Cathy McCarthy
Music Consultant & Audio Examples: Sal Grillo

Cover Art Direction & Design:
Jimmy Rutkowski

HL00109244
ISBN: 978-1-4768-6760-1

Table of Contents

Words from the Author

To learn a new language you take small steps, progressively increasing your knowledge until you speak it fluidly. Music is the language you are learning. With consistent practice this book will take you to the next level, attaining your goal to play music. In this book you will learn the important basics to build a solid foundation of music. Don't just play; take time to listen to what you are playing as well as other musicians. When your ears hear and understand music, your fingers will respond. So let's get to our pianos, open our ears and mind and let's play music.

John McCarthy

Quick Start Video

Download this free video from our On Demand System at RockHouseSchool.com. It will help guide you through the important first steps of getting started with your piano.

Digital eBook

When you register this product at the lesson support site RockHouseSchool.com, you will receive a digital version of this book. This interactive eBook can be used on all devices that support Adobe PDF. This will allow you to access your book using the latest portable technology any time you want.

The Rock House Method Learning System

This learning system can be used on your own or guided by a teacher. Be sure to register for your free lesson support at RockHouseSchool.com. Your member number can be found inside the cover of this book.

Lesson Support Site: Once registered, you can use this fully interactive site along with your product to enhance your learning experience, expand your knowledge, link with instructors, and connect with a community of people around the world who are learning to play music using The Rock House Method®.

Gear Education Video: Walking into a music store can be an intimidating endeavor for someone starting out. To help you, Rock House has a series of videos to educate you on some of the gear you will encounter as you start your musical journey.

Quizzes: Each level of the curriculum contains multiple quizzes to gauge your progress. When you see a quiz icon go to the *Lesson Support* site and take the quiz. It will be graded and emailed to you for review.

Audio Examples & Play Along Tracks: Demonstrations of how each lesson should sound and full band backing tracks to play certain lessons over. These audio tracks are available on the accompanying mp3 CD.

Icon Key

These tell you there is additional information and learning utilities available at RockHouseSchool.com to support that lesson.

Backing Track

Backing track icons are placed on lessons where there is an audio demonstration to let you hear what that lesson should sound like or a backing track to play the lesson over. Use these audio tracks to guide you through the lessons. **This is an mp3 CD, it can be played on any computer and all mp3 disc compatible playback devices.**

Metronome

Metronome icons are placed next to the examples that we recommend you practice using a metronome. You can download a free, adjustable metronome on the *Lesson Support* site.

Worksheet

Worksheets are a great tool to help you thoroughly learn and understand music. These worksheets can be downloaded at the *Lesson Support* site.

Finger Numbers

As you play you will see finger numbers above and below the music. These indicate which finger to use to play that note. Both thumbs are number 1 and both pinkies are number 5.

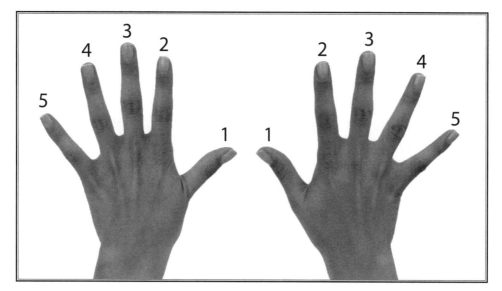

Posture & Hand Placement

You must build great habits right from the beginning. Having proper posture and hand placement will allow you to progress quickly.

Proper Posture

Sit facing the keyboard like the diagram below.

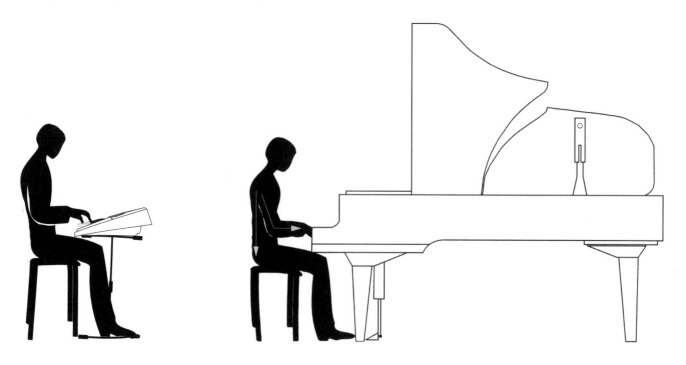

Hand Position

Arch your fingers so that your tips are going straight down in the middle of the keys and curve your thumb inward.

The Musical Alphabet

The musical alphabet consists of seven letters A through G. After G the letters loop back to A and start over again. There are no note names higher in the musical alphabet then G. These seven letters will be the names of the white keys on your keyboard.

A - B - C - D - E - F - G

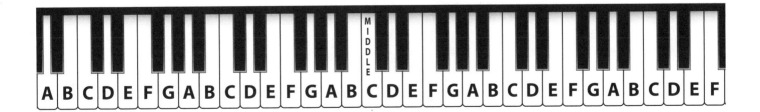

Finding Middle C

Middle C is the note that sits right in the middle of the keyboard and will be a starting point where you divide your left and right hands. You can use the black keys as a guide to find middle C. Locate the two black keys together in the middle of the keyboard, the white key just before the first black key is the middle C note.

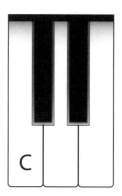

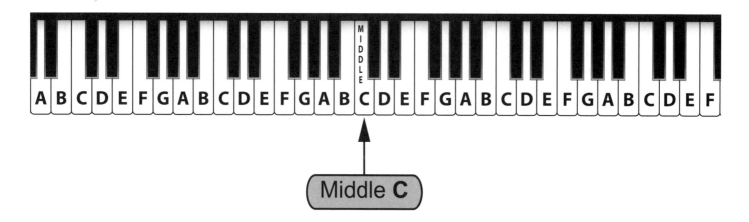

Middle **C**

Right Hand Notes Up from Middle C

Starting with your right hand thumb on the middle C note play five notes up the keyboard. As you play each note say the name out loud.

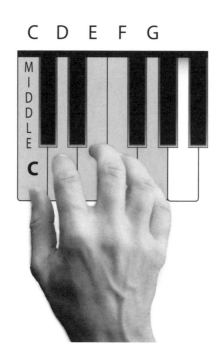

The Repeat Sign

A repeat sign (double line with two dots) signifies that all of the written music between the repeat signs is to be repeated.

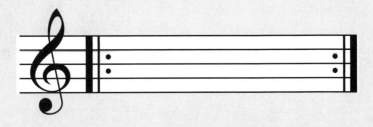

Right Hand Finger Pattern

CD Track 2-3

Here is a right hand pattern to help get your fingers ready to play songs. Make sure to use your finger tips playing one note at a time. Repeat the pattern for five minutes or until your hand gets tired. Practice like this will warm your hand up and build coordination.

$$\| : \quad C-D-E-F-G-F-E-D \quad : \|$$

Finger: 1   2   3   4   5   4   3   2

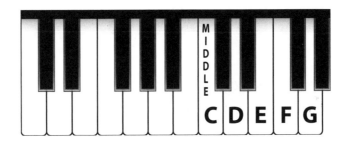

Left Hand Notes Down from Middle C

Starting with your left hand thumb on the middle C note play five notes down the keyboard. Start slow and build up speed gradually.

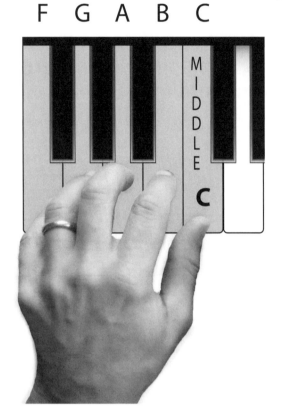

Left Hand Finger Pattern

CD Track

4-5

Here is a left hand pattern to help get your fingers ready to play songs. As you did with your right hand practice this pattern for five minutes a day or until your fingers get tired. As you play say the name of each note out loud. This will help you memorize the notes on your keyboard. Play the notes one at a time using your finger tips.

‖: **C - B - A - G - F - G - A - B** :‖

Finger:　1　　2　　3　　4　　5　　4　　3　　2

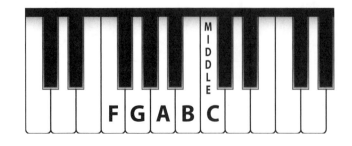

Black Key Groups of Two & Three

The black keys fall into a pattern. There are two together then three together all across the keyboard. This repetitive pattern will help you easily memorize the names of the notes across the keyboard.

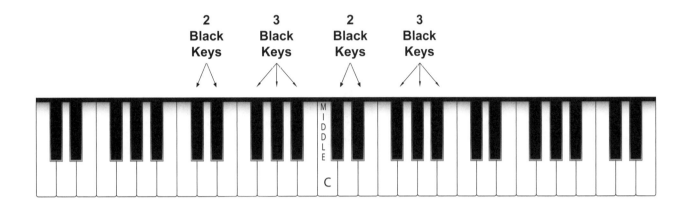

White Key Names Around Two Black Keys

The three white keys around the two black key group are C – D – E. Play these three notes across the keyboard.

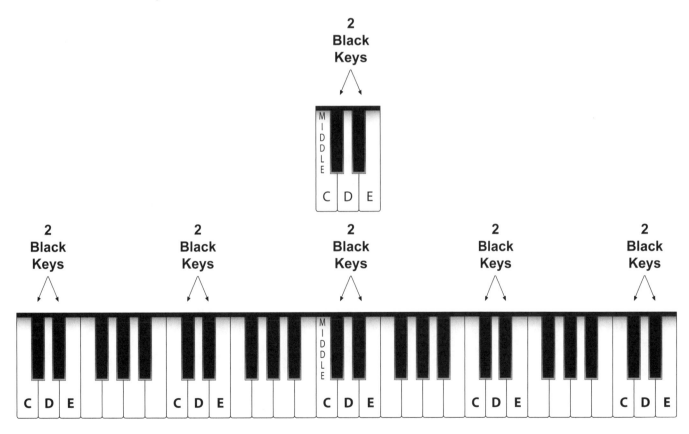

White Key Names Around Three Black Keys

The four white keys around the three black key group are F - G - A - B. Play these four notes across the keyboard. Memorize the note locations. This will help you as you learn songs.

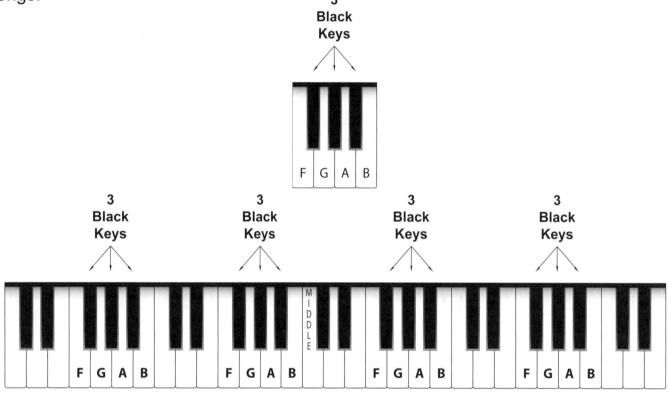

Locating Notes Across the Keyboard

Use the black keys as a guide to locate notes across the keyboard. Play each of the following notes across your keyboard and call out it's name.

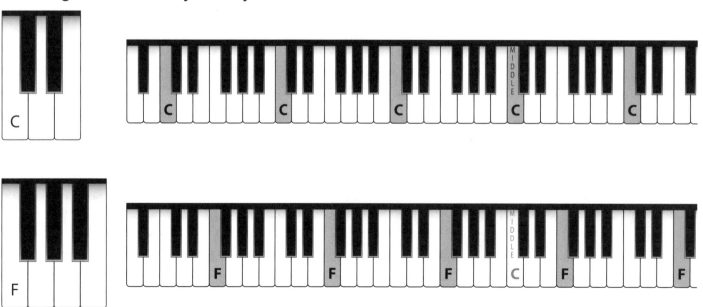

Treble Staff

Music is written on a **STAFF** consisting of **FIVE LINES** and **FOUR SPACES**. The lines and spaces are numbered as shown:

5th Line
————————————————————————————————————
                              4th Space
4th Line
————————————————————————————————————
                              3rd Space
3rd Line
————————————————————————————————————
                              2nd Space
2nd Line
————————————————————————————————————
                              1st Space
1st Line
————————————————————————————————————

The lines and spaces are named after letters of the alphabet. You can use the saying to memorize the names easily. The lines are named as follows:

5 ——————————————————(F)—————————————— Fine
4 ——————————————(D)—————————————————— Does
3 ————————————(B)———————————————————— Boy
2 ——————(G)—————————————————————————— Good
1 ——(E)—————————————————————————————— Every

The letter names of the spaces are F - A - C - E they spell the word "FACE."

4 ——————————————————————————E————————
3 ————————————————————C——————————————
2 ——————————————A————————————————————
1 ——————F————————————————————————————

F-A-C-E

13

Staff Symbols

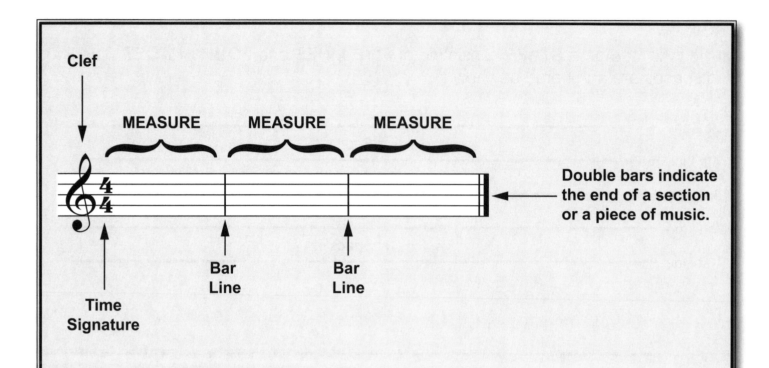

Measures & Bar Lines

The staff is divided into measures by vertical lines called bar lines.

Treble Clef

The second line of the treble clef is known as the G line. Some people call the treble clef the "G clef" because the tail circles around the G line of the staff.

Time Signature

Time signatures are written at the beginning of a piece of music. The top number tells you how many beats there are in each measure and the bottom number tells what type of beat is receiving the count.

Learn Piano 1 - Quiz 1

Once you complete this section go to RockHouseSchool.com and take the quiz to track your progress. You will receive an email with your results and suggestions.

Right Hand Notes on the Treble Staff

The next lessons will use these five notes played on the treble staff. Memorize these notes their name and which finger to play each with. In addition to the lines and spaces you learned I've added two lower notes D and middle C. Notice that the D is on the space below the first line and middle C is on a line below the staff. Notes on lines below or above the staff are placed on small lines called ledger lines. Play each note saying the name out loud and memorize these notes on your keyboard.

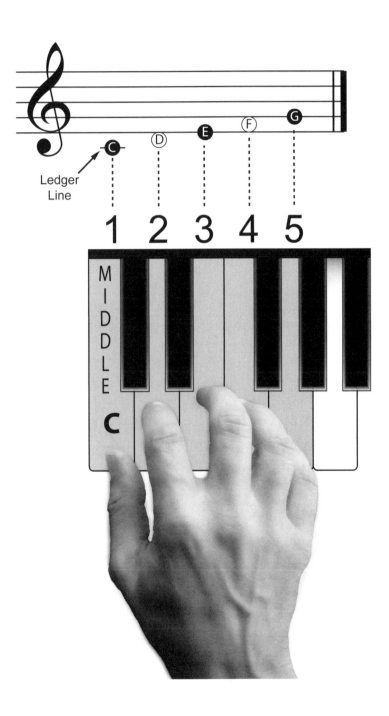

15

Note Values - Quarter, Half & Whole Notes

CD Track
6-8

Notes will tell you how long each note rings. Below are the first note types you will be using in this book. Play the examples for each note type below. Make sure to hold your finger pressed down on each note for the entire duration.

Whole Note = 4 Beats

A whole note has a hollow head and no stem and receives four beats or counts.

Count: 1   2   3   4

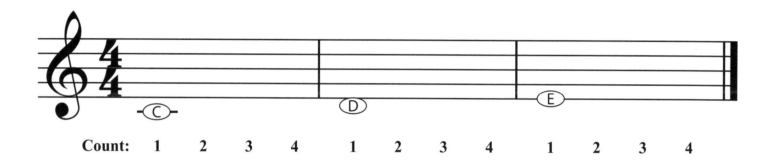

Count: 1   2   3   4   1   2   3   4   1   2   3   4

Half Note = 2 Beats

A half note has a hollow head and a stem and receives two beats, or counts.

Count: 1   2   3   4

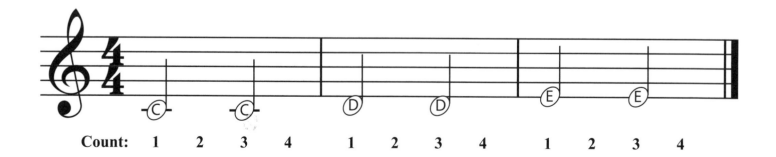

Count: 1   2   3   4   1   2   3   4   1   2   3   4

Quarter Note = 1 Beat

A quarter note has a solid head and a stem and receives one beat, or count.

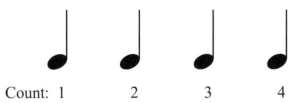

Count: 1   2   3   4

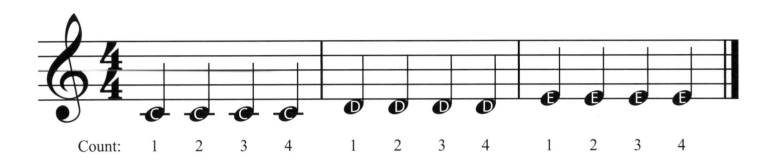

Count: 1 2 3 4   1 2 3 4   1 2 3 4

CD Track
9-10

Hot Cross Buns

As you practice this song pay attention to the timing and how long to let each note ring. You can count along as you play 1 - 2 - 3 - 4 for each measure. Start to memorize each notes location on the staff.

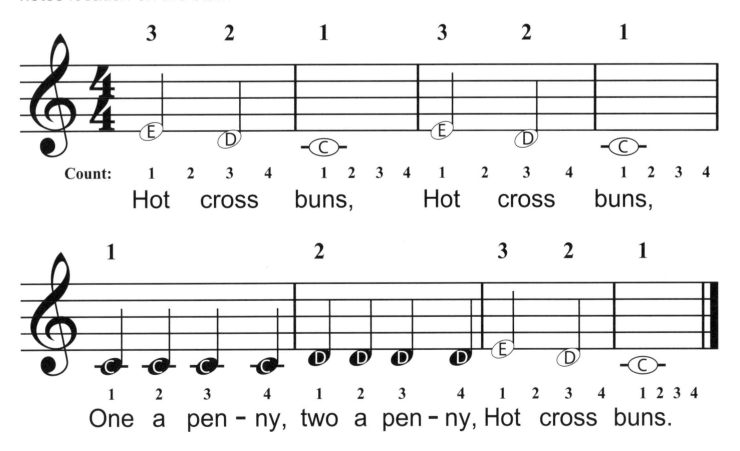

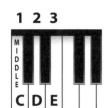

By the Silv'ery Moonlight

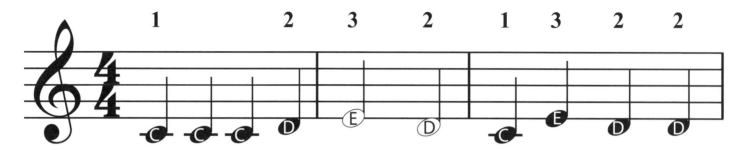

By the sil-v'ry moon-light, my dear friend Pier-

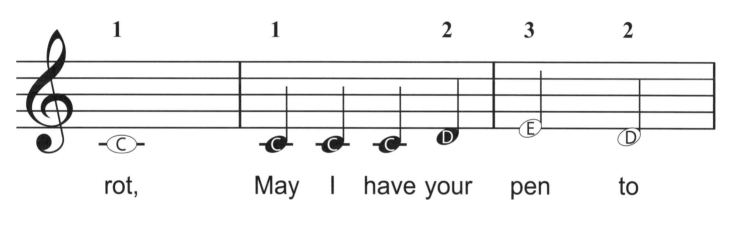

rot, May I have your pen to

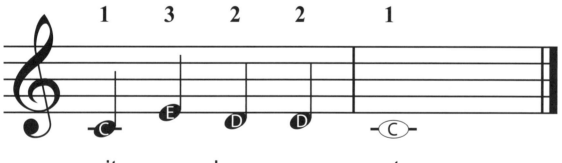

write my love a note.

Backing Tracks

CD Track Many of the songs songs in this book will have a backing track that you can play along with. These will be either audio demonstrations or full band tracks. This will help you learn to play with other musicians. The songs with backing tracks will be depicted with the CD track icon.

Rain Rain Go Away

You will now play the F and G notes. Make sure to use the proper finger to play each note.

Rain, rain, Go a - way.

Come a - gain some o - ther day

Key Dynamics

Dynamics in music is the difference between loud and soft. Many keyboards are dynamic and notes can be played louder or softer. On a piano the keys are velocity sensitive, this means the harder you hit the note the louder it will sound. Some electronic keyboards have touch sensitive keys as well but many electronic keyboards are not dynamic.

Go Tell Aunt Rhody

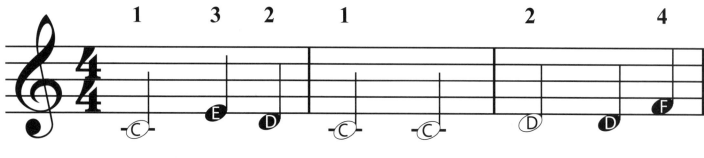

Go   tell Aunt   Rho - dy,   Go   tell Aunt

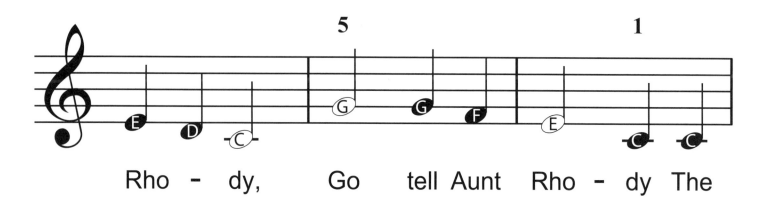

Rho - dy,   Go   tell Aunt   Rho - dy   The

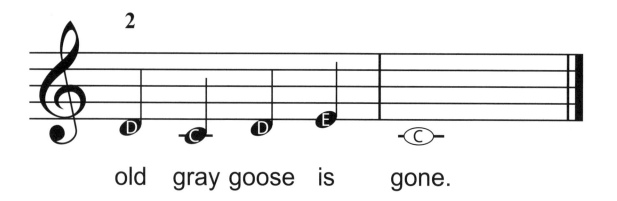

old   gray goose   is   gone.

The next songs will not have the letters inside the notes. As you play call the note names out loud to help memorize the notes. You must now learn the notes by location on the staff. Middle C is always on the line below the staff, D the space below the staff and E is on the bottom line.

Aura Lee

CD Track 17-18

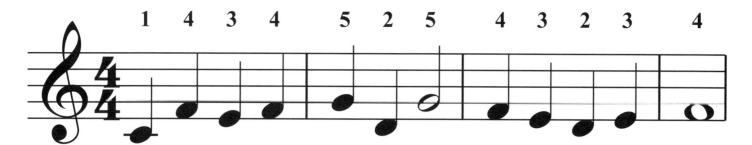

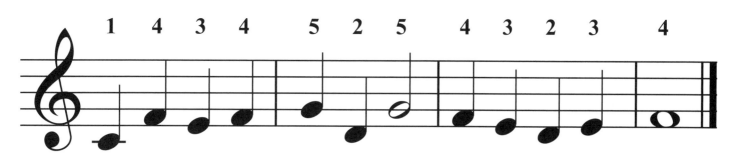

Jingle Bells

CD Track 19-21

Jin - gle bells!   Jin - gle bells jin - gle all the way!

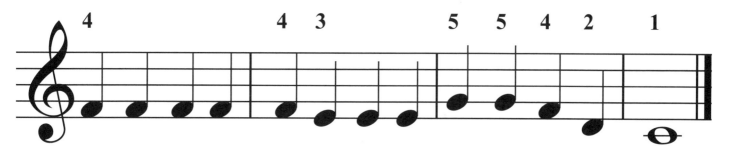

Oh what fun it   is to ride a one horse o - pen sleigh!

Good King Wenceslas

CD Track

22-24

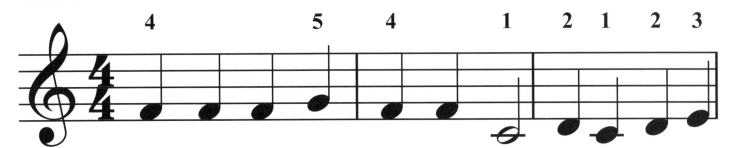

Good King Wen ces - las looked out, On the feast of

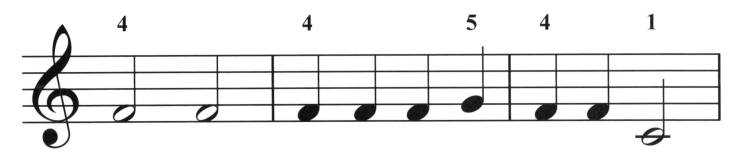

Ste - phen   When the snow lay   round a - bout,

Deep and crisp and   e - ven.

Metronome

A metronome is a device that clicks at an adjustable rate that you set. It is used to help develop a sense of timing and to help gauge your progress. By playing along with the clicking sound you get the sense of playing with another musician. Each click represents one beat; a common way to count beats is to tap your foot. One beat would equal tapping your foot down up. Play all the songs and exercises in this book along with a metronome. If you don't have a metronome you can download one for free at the *Lesson Support* site.

White Key Finger Flexing

CD Track
25-28

Now, let's get your fingers moving on the keyboard. The following are a series of warm up exercises to get your fingers coordinated and ready to play more complicated music. The numbers represent the finger you will use to play each note. Look at the diagram to see which key each finger aligns with. Just like athletes warm up before games musicians should warm up before playing for peak performance.

Right Hand

Example 1

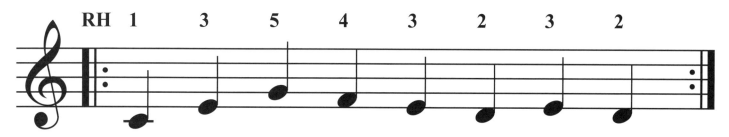

Example 2

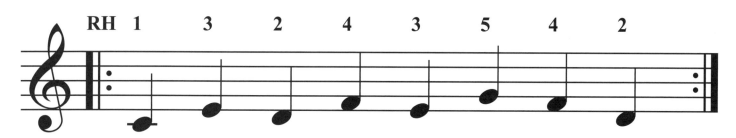

Pick Up Notes

When there is an incomplete measure starting a song these notes are called "pick up notes." When this occurs the last measure will also be incomplete; but, the combination of both together will equal a full measure. When counting into the song still count the full count but just start later.

23

A Tisket, a Tasket

Count:
1 2 3 4 - 1   2   3   4

A tis - ket, a   tas - ket, a green and yel - low bas - ket, I

wrote a let - ter   to my love, and on the way I dropped   it.

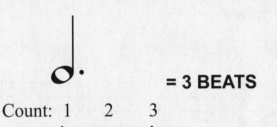

Dotted Half Notes

A dotted half note receives three beats or counts. It is a regular half note with a dot placed after it.

= 3 BEATS

Count: 1   2   3

3/4 Timing

Here is a new time signature that will be used in the next song. In 3/4 time there is three beats per measure. This timing is used in many songs.

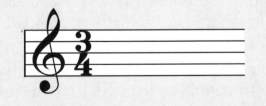

I Saw Three Ships

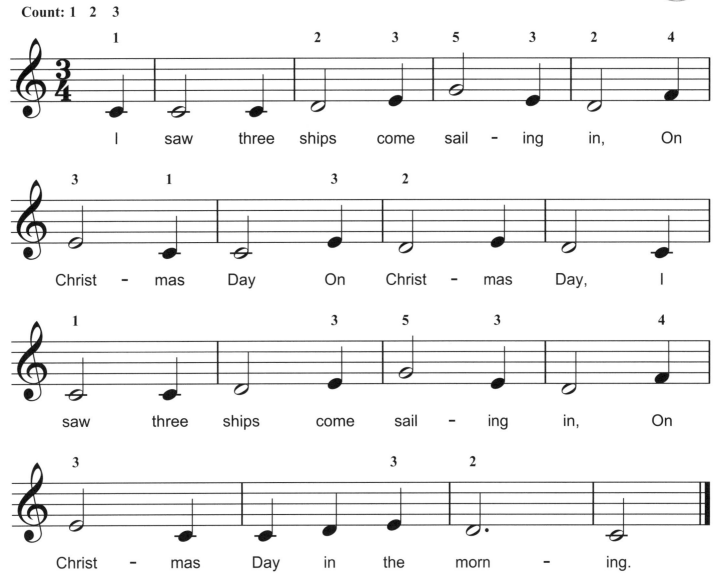

Count: 1 2 3

I saw three ships come sail - ing in, On

Christ - mas Day On Christ - mas Day, I

saw three ships come sail - ing in, On

Christ - mas Day in the morn - ing.

Rests

The next melody contains your first rests. A rests is a period of silence. Like whole, half and quarter notes you keep time only there is no sound. See what each rest looks like below.

Whole Note Rest	Half Note Rest	Quarter Note Rest
4 Beats	2 Beats	1 Beat

Oh, When the Saints

Oh, when the saints, Go march-ing in.

Oh, when the saints go march - ing in.

Oh, Lord I want to be in that numb - er.

When the saints go march - ing in.

Dynamics in Music

As you are playing a song there will often be symbols that tell you what dynamic level to play the song. The dynamic level is how loud or soft the song should be played. The following are common symbols used for dynamics.

p - Piano, meaning soft

mp - Mezzo-piano, meaning medium soft

mf - Mezzo-forte, meaning medium loud

f - Forte, meaning loud

Fais Dodo

Away in the Forest

Count: 1 2 3 4

mf

A - way in the deep fo - rest, The o - wl hoots,"Yoo - hoo." While

from a grand old oak tree Re - plies the small cuc - koo: "Cuc -

koo, cuc - koo", Re - plies the small cuc - koo. "Cuc -

koo, cuc - koo", Re - plies the small cuc - koo.

The Tie

When notes on the **same** line or space are joined with a curved line, they are called tied notes. The note is only played once but will ring for the combined values of both notes.

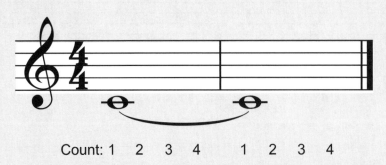

Count: 1 2 3 4   1 2 3 4

28

Left Hand Cross Over

At times you will need to cross your left hand over the right hand to play notes in order to make the song flow smoothly. I've outlined the three notes in the following song in which you will cross over and play with your left hand 2nd finger.

Row, Row, Row your Boat

CD Track

39-40

Row,   row,   row   your   boat,

mf

Gent – ly   down   the   stream,_____

L.H. Over

Mer – ri – ly   mer – ri – ly,   mer – ri – ly,   mer – ri – ly,

Life   is   but   a   dream._____

Learn Piano 1 - Quiz 2

Once you complete this section go to RockHouseSchool.com and take the quiz to track your progress. You will receive an email with your results and suggestions.

Bass Staff

The bass clef is used for music to be played with the left hand. It is also called the F clef because it circles around the F line.

This staff also has five lines and four spaces but the names will be different then the treble clef. The lines on the staff are G – B – D – F – A. A saying that will help you memorize these lines are Good – Boys – Do – Fine – Always. Look below at all the notes across the bass staff.

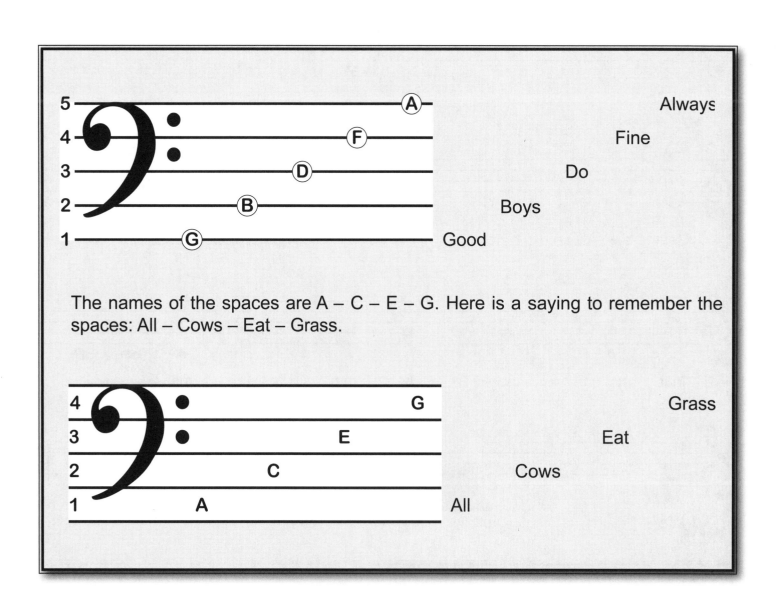

The names of the spaces are A – C – E – G. Here is a saying to remember the spaces: All – Cows – Eat – Grass.

Left Hand Notes on the Bass Staff

The next lessons will use these five notes played on the bass staff. Memorize these notes their name and which finger to play each with.

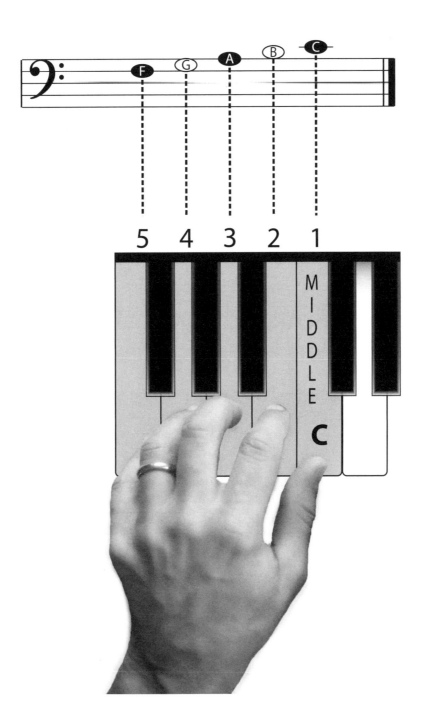

In the next two songs you will play using only your left hand. Memorize the notes because you will combine both hands playing songs soon.

Lefty Lucy

Move to the Left

Left Hand Finger Flexing

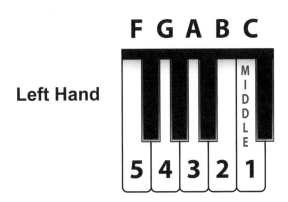

Left Hand

F G A B C

5 4 3 2 1

Example 1

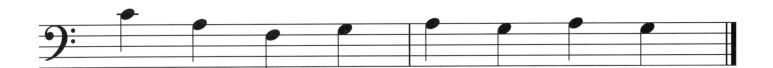

Example 2

The Grand Staff

Piano music is written on a grand staff. This staff combines the treble and bass staffs together. They are connected by bar lines and a brace.

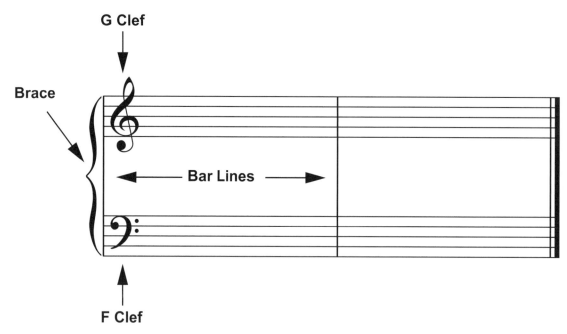

Below are the notes on the grand staff. Use the diagram so you can see where they fall on your keyboard.

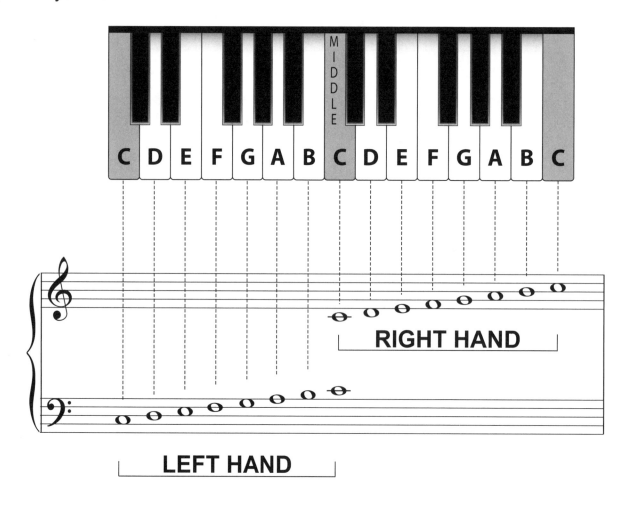

Two Thumbs on C

Now you will play using both hands together. Look below to see the proper way to place your hands on the keyboard.

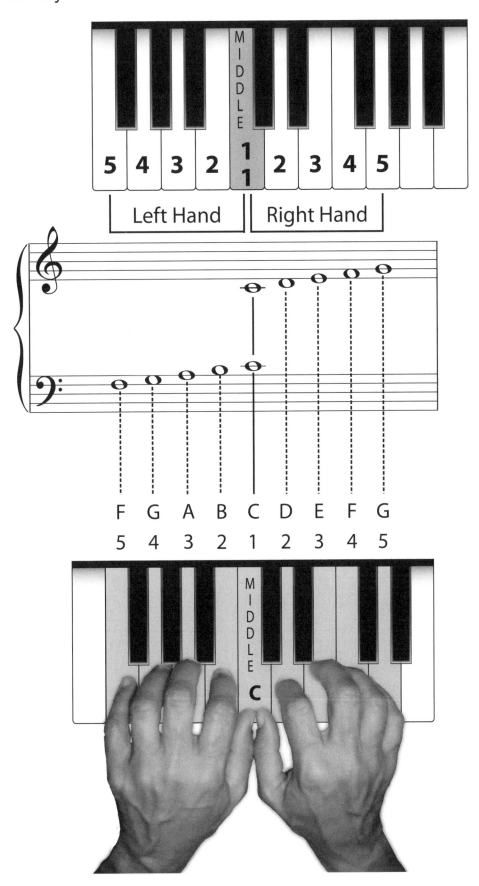

Reading Two Staffs

Now you will be reading two staffs together. The bottom bass staff will be played with your left hand and the top treble staff will be played with your right hand. It will take time and practice to read music this way so be patient. Start each song at a slow pace and build speed gradually.

Yankee Doodle

CD Track
49-50

Here is your first song playing notes with both hands. Take your time and pay attention to the finger numbers to make this song easier to play. The fingers on both hands should always be on the keys in position to play notes.

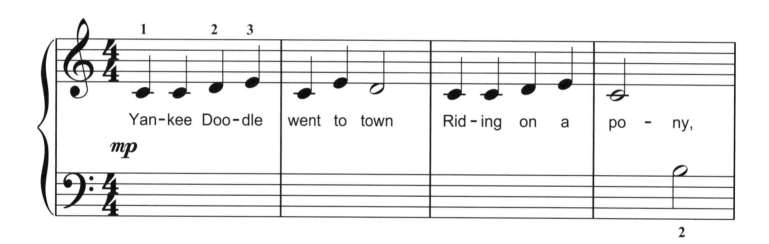

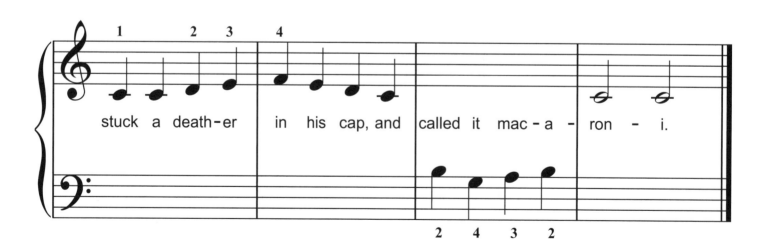

London Bridge

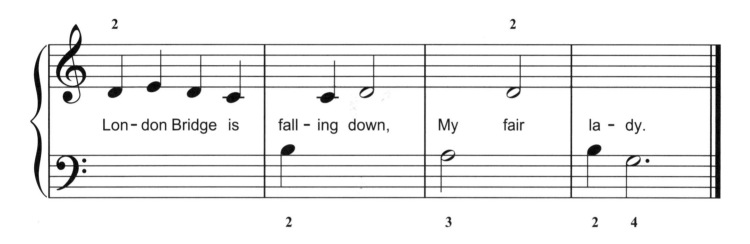

Tempo

Tempo is the speed in which music is played. It is measured in beats per minute or bpm. There will be tempo setting at the beginning of many songs that require a specific tempo. Here are some of the most common tempo settings:

Adagio - Slow - 66 - 76 bpm

Andante - Moderately Slow - 76 - 108 bpm

Moderato - Moderate - 108 - 120 bpm

Allegro - Fast - 120 - 168 bpm

Twinkle Twinkle Little Star

Andante

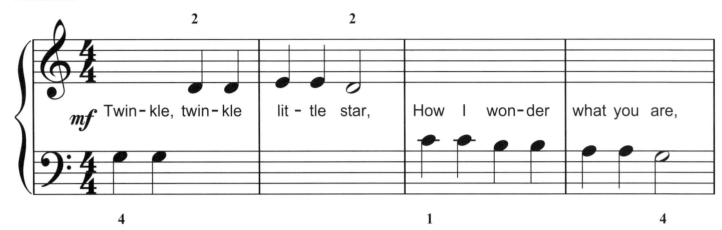

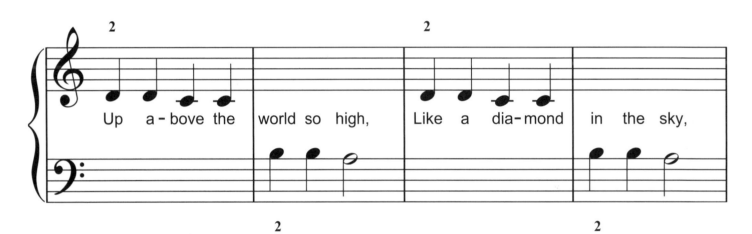

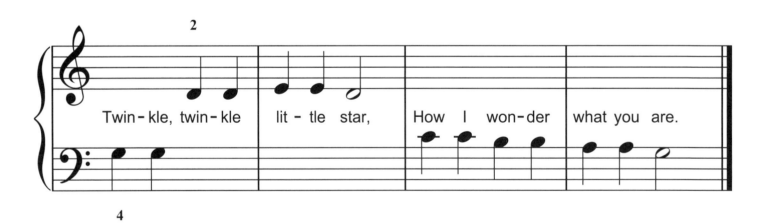

Jolly Old Saint Nicholas

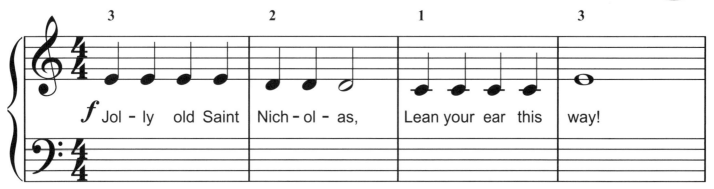

Moderato

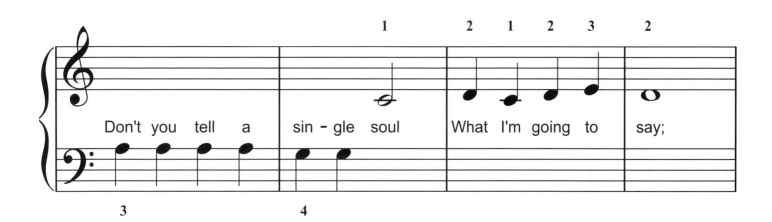

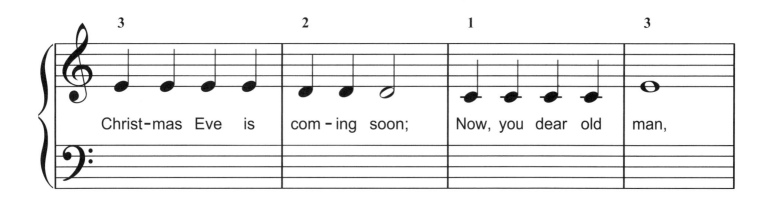

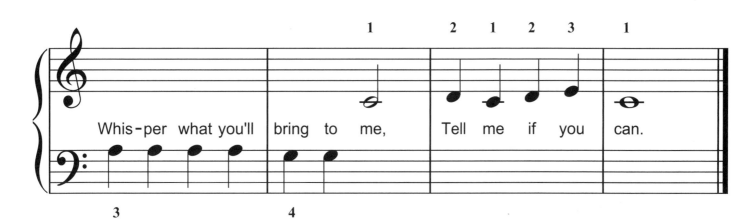

39

Camptown Races

Moderato

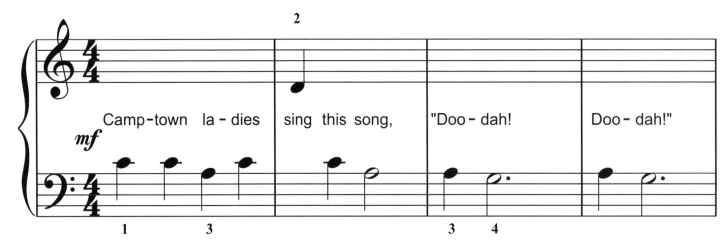

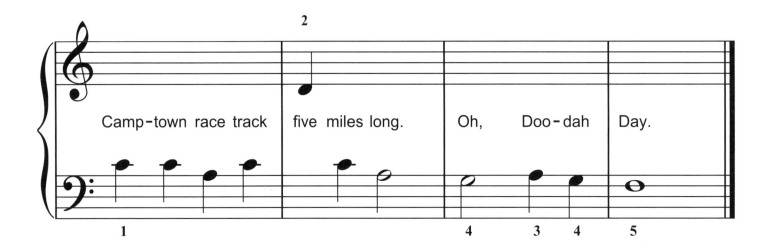

Ritardando

Ritardando (or rit.) is a musical term that means a section of music is to gradually slow down. It is written in music with the letters rit. followed by a dashed horizontal line indicating the length. This can add emotion to a song.

Two Hands Together

From this point on, the songs will require you to play notes with both hands together at times. This requires practice and concentration. You should isolate any sections that you have difficulty with and practice them repetitively. "Repetition is the mother of skill."

Bingo

CD Track
62-63

The last two measures of this song have a ritardando. Slow the tempo down to make a dramatic ending.

Moderato

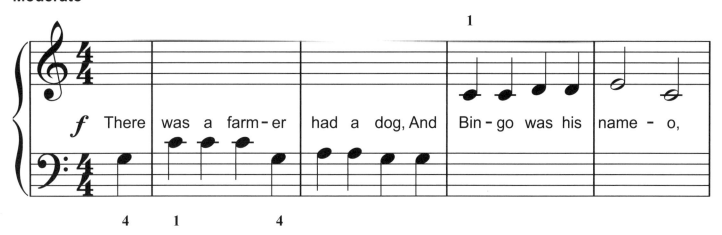

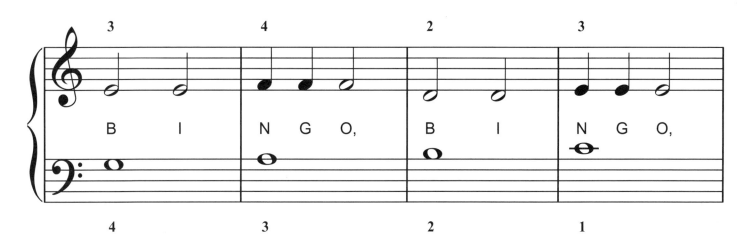

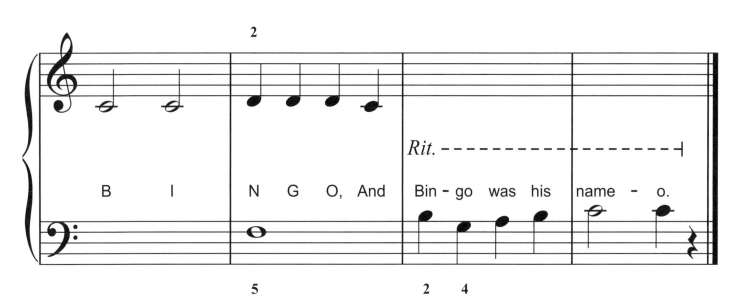

We Three Kings

CD Track
64-65

Andante

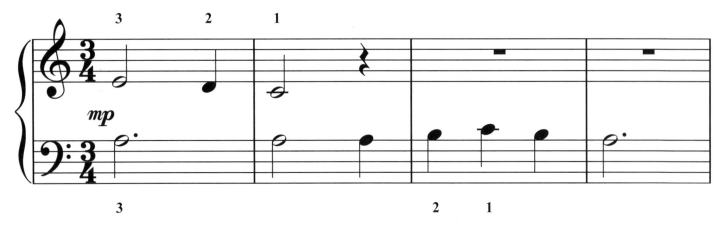

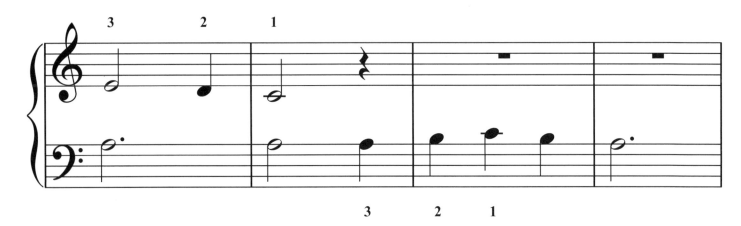

Left Hand C Position Notes

Here are the left hand C position notes on the bass staff. Play through these notes and memorize them. You will be combining both hands to play in C position in the coming lessons.

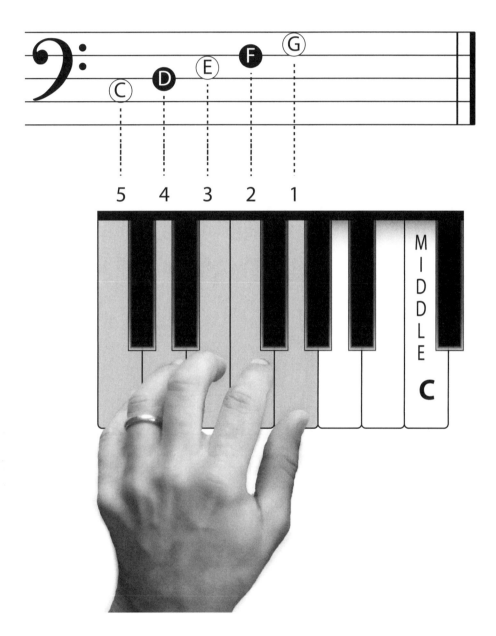

The next two songs you will play using only your left hand in C position. Memorize where the notes are on the staff and their names. Say the name of each note out loud as you play to help learn effectively.

Aura Lee

CD Track
66-67

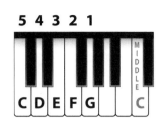

Ode To Joy

CD Track
68-69

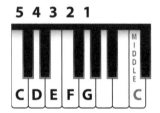

C Position Both Hands

The next lessons will contain music written in what's called "C Position." This is a starting point that you will place both hands on the keyboard to play the music effectively. There will be some notes outside this region that you will need to play as well. Below are the C position notes on the grand staff. Use the diagram so you can see where they fall on your keyboard. Play them and call the note names out loud.

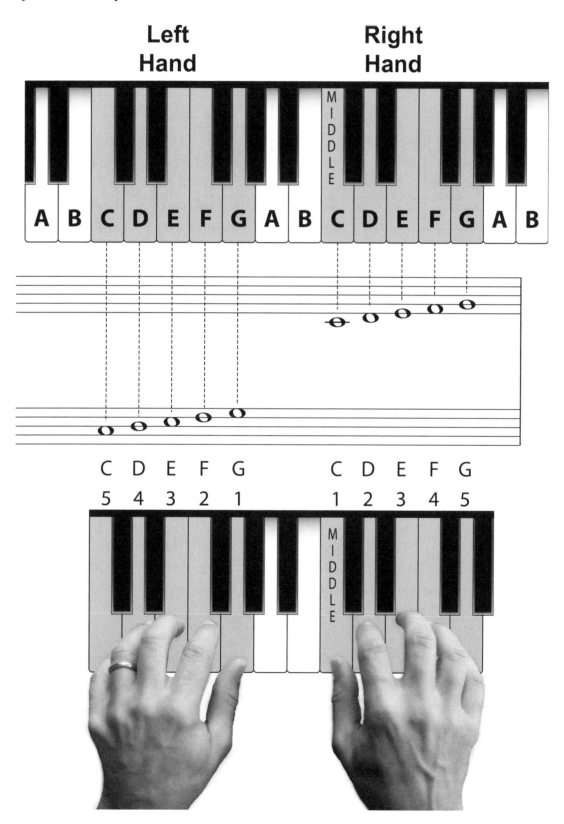

Etude with Two Hands

The following songs will be played in C position using both hands. Pay close attention to the fingering there will be some notes that will be played extending the position notes. This C hand position is just a starting point to give you a base but as you progress you will expand your note knowledge to play the entire keyboard.

Andante

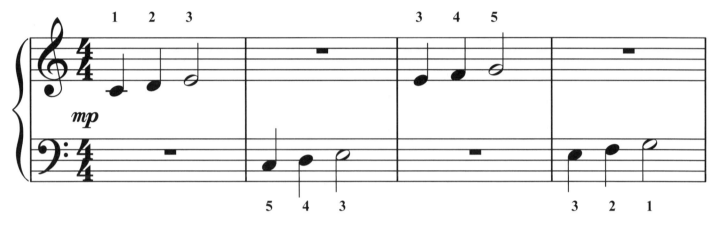

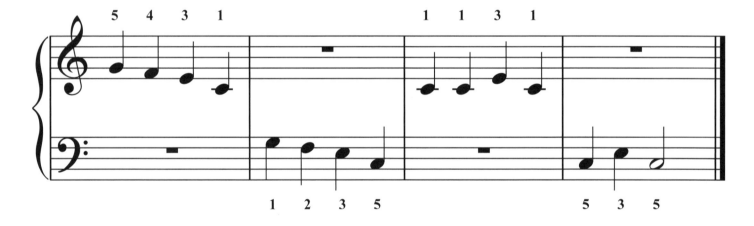

Expanding Your Note Reach

In the next song your left hand will play notes from C up to A. Position your left hand one key higher then the C position so your 1st finger can play the A note. You will shift back down to C position to play the last note C. In the coming songs you will also expand to play more notes with your right hand. Pay close attention to the fingering.

Old MacDonald

Moderato

My Melody

Moderato

Run Away Train

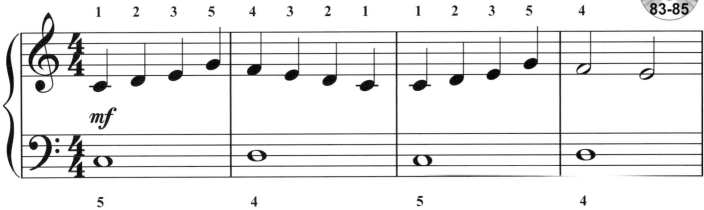

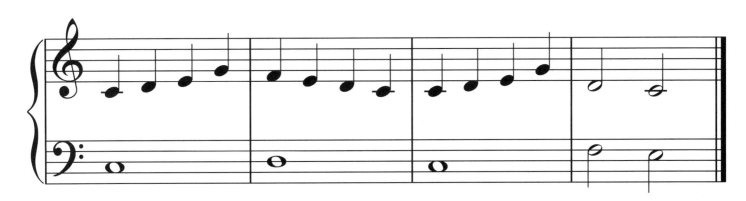

Bottoms Up

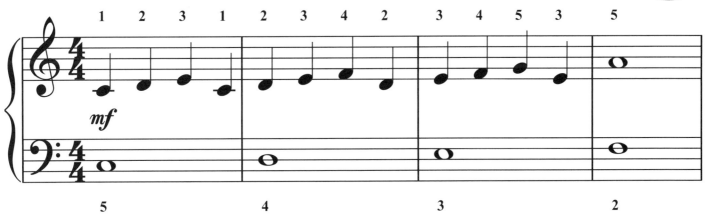

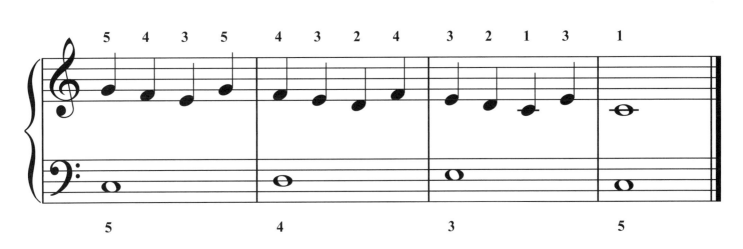

Surprise Symphony

In this next song, there will be a new note introduced. It is the B note that is played one white key below middle C with your right hand first finger. The B note is shown in the diagram above as well as marked in gray on the staff below.

Practice Tips

- Make sure to review previous lessons. A good idea is to review the past songs as a warm up before you start your new lesson.

- Use a metronome when practicing. Always start at a slow speed and increase your tempo once you can play the speed you are at comfortably.

- Record yourself if you have the capacity. When you listen back you will be more objective to any inconsistencies. Learn to be your own biggest critic.

Oh, When the Saints

Count: 1 2 3 4 - 1 **2** **3** **4** 5

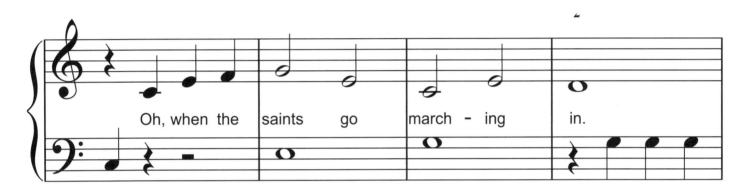

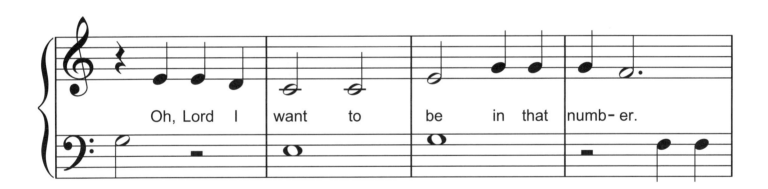

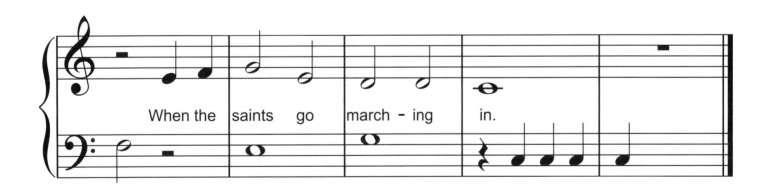

Learn Piano 1 - Quiz 3

Congratulations you've made it to the end of Book 1! Go to RockHouseSchool. com and take the quiz to track your progress. You will receive an email with your results and an official Rock House Method "Certificate of Completion" when you pass.

Appendix

Word Search

Go to RockHouseSchool.com to get the solution to this word search.

```
M N F U M Y E H G I I M O A N J Z A E U W R M A E
G I I F F Z N V X R E N P U G C M D I T H O J T M
F R N T A H C R J A P U M Z M J I I T U Z M O P N
M I Y R B T R D S W L X E T H K I M D J V N L M T
D E S U N N S U B K D L T K H Z T D E D P B Q Z V
Y C T Q D O R E T J Y A W Y T K R O N U L E W G N
N J A R V E R I L W I P S R N A K L K N C E P D S
A W N I O U D M C B J S U C O S V C M P C G C M V
M V B I T N E G E P E U S B T Z I B L A C K K E Y
I E A S O D O T J D B R Y Q Y P K T I Y N H N L F
C X R Z P Z O M D V T E T Q V T I M I N G C A R N
S Q X Y F N M X E O K S F D T Q E J V J D G J R Y
X N E T F Q Y I J Y P L S X B I S N V O J M F T D
K C L L K S W W H O L E N O T E F F A T S S S A B
G P A J A U T E E I X B E Q Q H L H I G T Y W M P
Y H O O K R X A B J Q T S E R Z F Y A U I F L Y V
W H I T E K E Y F C A S G Y P D T G G N Z C E T S
F F M E C Z I H X F J A A L M K W E T Q J H Y R W
L T R T K M D Q A X Y A S Q S C R K M U Y X O D D
P U X Z B S G P K M A L W N W E X U A B J D Z L W
```

Search Words:

- BASS STAFF
- BLACK KEY
- DYNAMICS
- HALF NOTE
- KEYBOARD
- MEASURE
- METRONOME
- MIDDLE C
- PICKUP NOTE

- REST
- STAFF
- TEMPO
- TIE
- TIMING
- TREBLE STAFF
- WHITE KEY
- WHOLE NOTE

Chord
Glossary

A

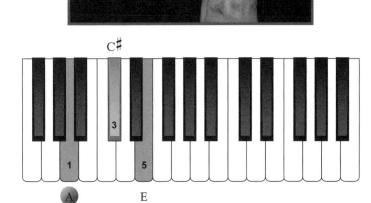

Am

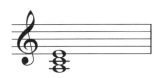

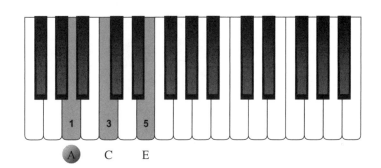

B

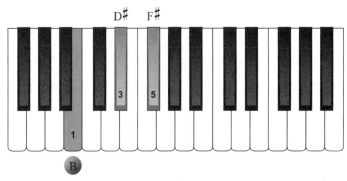

Bm

C

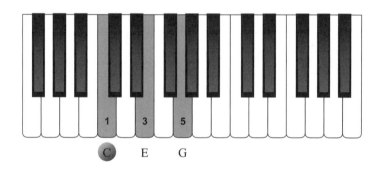

Cm

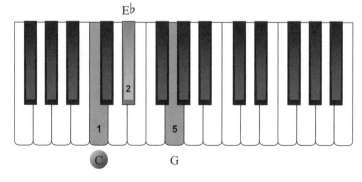

56

D

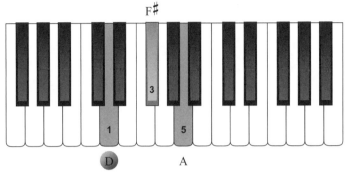

F#

3

1   5

D   A

Dm

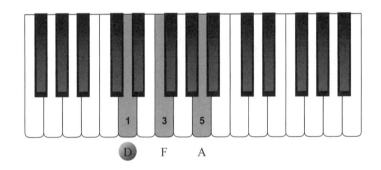

1   3   5

D   F   A

E

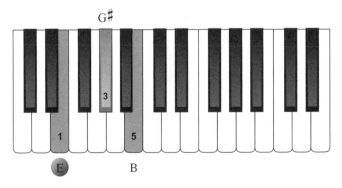

G#

3

1   5

E   B

Em

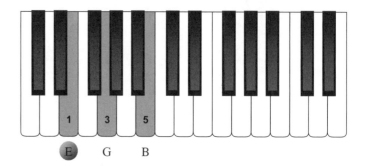

F

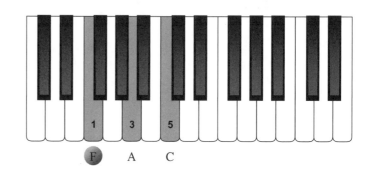

Fm

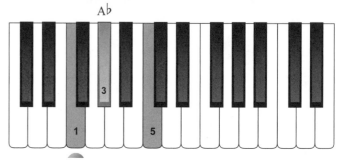

G

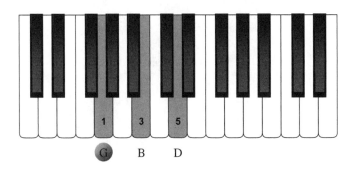

Gm

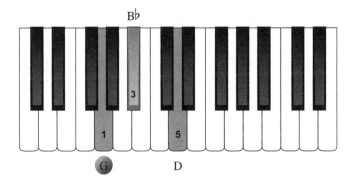

About the Author

John McCarthy
Creator of
The Rock House Method

John is the creator of **The Rock House Method®**, the world's leading musical instruction system. Over his 20 plus year career, he has produced and/or appeared in more than 100 instructional products. Millions of people around the world have learned to play music using John's easy-to-follow, accelerated program.

John is a virtuoso musician who has worked with some of the industry's most legendary entertainers. He has the ability to break down, teach and communicate music in a manner that motivates and inspires others to achieve their dreams of playing an instrument. As a musician and songwriter, John blends together a unique style of rock, funk and blues in a collage of melodic compositions.

Throughout his career, John has recorded and performed with renowned musicians like Doug Wimbish (who's worked with Joe Satriani, Living Colour, The Rolling Stones, Madonna, Annie Lennox and many more top flight artists), Grammy Winner Leo Nocentelli, Rock & Roll Hall of Fame inductees Bernie Worrell and Jerome "Big Foot" Brailey, Freekbass, Gary Hoey, Bobby Kimball, David Ellefson (founding member of seven time Grammy nominee Megadeth), Will Calhoun (who's worked with B.B. King, Mick Jagger and Paul Simon), Jordan Giangreco from the acclaimed band The Breakfast, and solo artist Alex Bach. John has also shared the stage with Blue Oyster Cult, Randy Bachman, Marc Rizzo, Jerry Donahue, Bernard Fowler, Stevie Salas, Brian Tichy, Kansas, Al Dimeola and Dee Snyder.

To get more information and about John McCarthy, his music and instructional products visit RockHouseSchool.com.